FASTING

THE PRIVATE DISCIPLINE
THAT BRINGS PUBLIC REWARD

acknowledgement

When a person begins any writing project, he almost always embarks on that venture with a need for help. As I approached this particular endeavor, there were numerous people that made themselves available to insure its success. I thank God for each of you and the contributions that you have made.

I want to extend special thanks to:

Dr. Rich Rogers and his unwavering commitment from start to finish.

Leah Cagle for her wise and insightful contributions.

My faithful staff at Free Chapel who are always willing to do whatever it takes "And Then Some!"

My loving wife Cherise and our five children, nothing on earth can compare to the blessing I have in you.

My prayer is that this fasting guide will bless all who desire a closer walk with HIM!

table of contents

small group information......................................6

week one..9

week two...............................,,,,,,,, ...31

week three.....................................53

week four......................................75

week five......................................97

Small Groups Building Relationships with purpose

A small group helps to create an environment that allows a person to connect with God and with others. A small group is the best way for sustained life-change to occur. An environment is created where real life issues are discussed and real-life relationships are formed. This is a place to pray and care for one another.

We encourage you to become involved in a small group or to start one as you go through these five weeks of fasting. It will change your life. This is the example that Jesus lead for us to follow.

How do you start a small group? Invite over a few of your friends, co-workers, family members or neighbors. Put in the small groups DVD and have everyone turn to the appropriate week in their study guide.

What's next? As a group, go through and ask questions from the question bank provided in the study. Begin a group discussion and the rest will follow.

As you can see a small group is very easy to start and to lead.

We have provided a few additional tips that will help you to build these relationships with purpose:

LEADER

Lead – *Lead your group by putting in the DVD and asking the questions in the study guide.*

Encourage – *Encourage others in your group to pray and participate.*

Allow – *Allow everyone the opportunity to get involved in the group discussions.*

Dedicate – *Dedicate yourself to praying and fasting for your group members.*

Enjoy – *Enjoy the time you spend in your small group.*

Relax – *Relax, you are going to be a great small group leader.*

Frequently Asked Questions

What is a small group? A small group consists of 8-10 people that meet to build relationships with purpose.

When does a small group meet? You and your group decide when you meet. We suggest that through this series you meet at least every other week, but it would be most beneficial to meet every week for the entire five week fasting guide.

Where does a small group meet? Small groups can choose to meet anywhere they would like. You can meet at a coffee shop, a restaurant or in someone's home.

Why is a small group important? It's important because God said it was (Acts 2:42-47) and Jesus lived it with His twelve disciples.

WEEK

Fasting for your breakthrough

As the deer pants for the water brooks
So my soul pants for you, O God.
My soul thirsts for God, for the living God.
When shall I come and appear before God?
My tears have been my food day and night,
While they continually say to me,
"Where is your God?"

—King David
[Psalm 42:1-3 NKJV]

Jesus, while being a very public figure, was actually a very private person. He is not seen praying in public nearly as much as He is seen praying in private. In fact, our Savior was so committed to prayer that He would often pray for hours on end, even through the night. He seemed to crave intimate moments alone with His father in heaven. Out of those private and profound times with His Father came an enormous outpouring of public demonstration. God's power would be poured forth in healings, raising the dead, and more. Victories are not won in public. This is why fasting, whether corporately or individually, is a private discipline. If you are ready to bring supernatural blessings into your life and release the power of God to overcome any situation, begin making the discipline of fasting a part of your life today. God is not a respecter of persons. What He has done in our church and in the lives of our members, He will do for you when you set your heart to seek Him through fasting.

Jentezen Franklin

As important and intriguing as divine depths might be, they defy discovery by the natural means of our minds. He reserves these things for those whose hearts are completely His...for those who take the time to wait before Him. Only in that way can there be intimacy with the Almighty. Tragically, precious little in this hurried and hassled age promotes such intimacy. We have become a body of people who look more like a herd of cattle in a stampede than a flock of God beside green pastures and still waters. Our forefathers knew, it seems, how to communicate with the Almighty, but do we? We must learn anew to think deeply, to worship meaningfully, to meditate unhurriedly.

Charles Swindoll
Intimacy with the Almighty

The purpose for week 1:

Fasting brings one into a deeper, more intimate and powerful relationship with the LORD. When you eliminate food from your diet for a number of days, your spirit becomes uncluttered by the things of this world and amazingly sensitive to things of God. As David stated in Psalm 42, "Deep calls unto deep." Week 1 is that first step on the path to your breakthrough. The first step is, many times, the hardest step, but as you walk through this journey with your small group you will find that God is there at every point along the way.

The goals for week 1 you will begin to:

Develop new relationships and/or strengthen already existing relationships within your group.

Develop an understanding of fasting.

Establish encouragement and accountability with in your group as you embark on this journey together

Identify your own personal reasons for fasting

Discover your God-given assignment and trust Him with the dreams that only He can make happen.

Notes:

_____

_____

_____

_____

_____

_____

_____

_____

Key Principle:

Every assignment has a birthplace. When God places a dream inside of you that only He can make possible, you need to fast and pray. Good or bad, what is within you will come out only as you fast and pray.

Group Discussion: Questions

 What is fasting? Have each member of your group explain what they understand fasting to mean. Have each member share what the Lord has laid on his or her heart to fast.

_____

_____

_____

_____

 What will you need from your group to help you successfully complete this 21-day fast?

_____

_____

_____

_____

 What has caused you to take this leap of faith?

_____

_____

_____

_____

 In the text, Pastor Franklin discusses several reasons Christians fast. Which of the following most accurately describes your reasons?
- Need for open doors (p. 13)
- Need for miraculous provision (p. 13)
- Need for the touch of God in your life (p. 13)

- Fulfillment of your God-given dreams (p. 13)
- Need of a fresh encounter with God (p. 14)
- Need of a deeper relationship with the Lord (p. 21)
- Need of sensitivity to the things of God (p. 21)
- Bondages that need to broken (p. 23)
- Salvation of a friend or loved one
- Desire to know God's will for your life (p. 27)
- Need of healing in your physical body
- Other

_____

_____

_____

_____

 On page 13 in the text, Pastor Franklin states that, "Every assignment has a birthplace. When God has placed a dream inside of you that only He can make possible, you need to fast and pray." Is there an assignment that God has given to you? Is there a dream that only He can make possible? Please write and share your answer with the group.

_____

_____

_____

_____

 Write and share with your group what you want to be able to say about yourself in next week's meeting.

_____

_____

_____

_____

Steps of action:

Exchange phone numbers of at least two other members of your group who will encourage and hold you accountable during the next week.

Identify your prayer time and place for the duration of your fast.

Pray and watch to see the activity of the Lord over the next few weeks. Take time daily to record your experiences in your prayer journal, this is a critical step in the process. When the fast is over, it will be important for you to look back and see the hand of God in your life over this 21-day period.

Make at least two phone calls this week to members of your small group to encourage them in this journey.

Final Thoughts:

God has a specific plan and purpose for your life. He desires that you:

Develop a deep and intimate relationship with your Lord and Savior Jesus Christ.

Discover the specific assignment He has for you, placing a dream in your heart that only He can make possible.

Hunger and thirst for Him more than you do food and water.

Experience breakthroughs, answered prayers, and intimacy with the Almighty that only fasting and prayer can produce.

Hear Him say, "Well done my good and faithful servant!" when our time on earth is through.

For further study: Matthew 6:1-18; Psalms 42:1-3; Ecclesiastes 4:12; Luke 5:34-35 & 6:40; I Peter 2:21

day one

As the deer pants for the water brooks So my soul pants for you, O God. My soul thirsts for God, for the living God. When shall I come and appear before God? My tears have been my food day and night, While they continually say to me, "Where is your God?"   —Psalm 42:1-3 NKJV

Focus on the Word

Meditate on the Word of God. Record your thoughts or what you believe the scripture is speaking to you.

_____

_____

_____

_____

Activate Your Praise

Record your praise reports. Give God praise for who He is.

_____

_____

_____

_____

Record your thanks for what God has done in your life.

_____

_____

_____

_____

Search your heart

Search me, O God, and know my heart; Try me, and know my anxieties;
And see if there is any wicked way in me, And lead me in the way everlasting.
—Psalms 139:23-24 NKJV

Admit any sin in your life - your shortcomings, faults and disappointments.

_____
_____
_____
_____

Target your prayers
I am praying for:

_____
_____
_____
_____

I am fasting for:

_____
_____
_____
_____

Listen and record His response to your prayers:

_____
_____
_____
_____

The best of all medicines is resting and fasting.
—Benjamin Franklin

day two

As the deer pants for the water brooks So my soul pants for you, O God. My soul thirsts for God, for the living God. When shall I come and appear before God? My tears have been my food day and night, While they continually say to me, "Where is your God?" —Psalm 42:1-3 NKJV

Focus on the Word

Meditate on the Word of God. Record your thoughts or what you believe the scripture is speaking to you.

_____

_____

_____

_____

Activate Your Praise

Record your praise reports. Give God praise for who He is.

_____

_____

_____

_____

Record your thanks for what God has done in your life.

_____

_____

_____

Search your heart

Search me, O God, and know my heart; Try me, and know my anxieties; And see if there is any wicked way in me, And lead me in the way everlasting. —Psalms 139:23-24 NKJV

Admit any sin in your life - your shortcomings, faults and disappointments.

_____

_____

_____

_____

Target your prayers
I am praying for:

_____

_____

_____

_____

I am fasting for:

_____

_____

_____

_____

Listen and record His response to your prayers:

_____

_____

_____

_____

I humbled my soul with fasting...
                    —*Psalm 35:13 NAS*

day three

As the deer pants for the water brooks So my soul pants for you, O God. My soul thirsts for God, for the living God. When shall I come and appear before God? My tears have been my food day and night, While they continually say to me, "Where is your God?"   —Psalm 42:1-3 NKJV

Focus on the Word

Meditate on the Word of God. Record your thoughts or what you believe the scripture is speaking to you.

_____

_____

_____

_____

Activate Your Praise

Record your praise reports. Give God praise for who He is.

_____

_____

_____

_____

Record your thanks for what God has done in your life.

_____

_____

_____

_____

Search your heart

Search me, O God, and know my heart; Try me, and know my anxieties; And see if there is any wicked way in me, And lead me in the way everlasting. —Psalms 139:23-24 NKJV

Admit any sin in your life - your shortcomings, faults and disappointments.

_____
_____
_____
_____

Target your prayers
I am praying for:

_____
_____
_____
_____

I am fasting for:

_____
_____
_____
_____

Listen and record His response to your prayers:

_____
_____
_____
_____

*Then Jehoshaphat feared, and set himself [determinedly, as his vital need]
to seek the Lord; he proclaimed a fast in all Judah.*
—2 Chronicles 20:3 AMP

day four

As the deer pants for the water brooks So my soul pants for you, O God. My soul thirsts for God, for the living God. When shall I come and appear before God? My tears have been my food day and night, While they continually say to me, "Where is your God?" —Psalm 42:1-3 NKJV

Focus on the Word

Meditate on the Word of God. Record your thoughts or what you believe the scripture is speaking to you.

Activate Your Praise

Record your praise reports. Give God praise for who He is.

Record your thanks for what God has done in your life.

Search your heart

Search me, O God, and know my heart; Try me, and know my anxieties; And see if there is any wicked way in me, And lead me in the way everlasting. —Psalms 139:23-24 NKJV

Admit any sin in your life - your shortcomings, faults and disappointments.

_____
_____
_____
_____

Target your prayers
I am praying for:

_____
_____
_____
_____

I am fasting for:

_____
_____
_____
_____

Listen and record His response to your prayers:

_____
_____
_____
_____

Fasting is a scriptural way to humble ourselves.
—Derek Prince, Fasting

day five

As the deer pants for the water brooks So my soul pants for you, O God. My soul thirsts for God, for the living God. When shall I come and appear before God? My tears have been my food day and night, While they continually say to me, "Where is your God?" —Psalm 42:1-3 NKJV

Focus on the Word

Meditate on the Word of God. Record your thoughts or what you believe the scripture is speaking to you.

_____
_____
_____
_____

Activate Your Praise

Record your praise reports. Give God praise for who He is.

_____
_____
_____
_____

Record your thanks for what God has done in your life.

_____
_____
_____
_____

Search your heart

Search me, O God, and know my heart; Try me, and know my anxieties; And see if there is any wicked way in me, And lead me in the way everlasting. —Psalms 139:23-24 NKJV

Admit any sin in your life - your shortcomings, faults and disappointments.

_____

_____

_____

_____

Target your prayers
I am praying for:

_____

_____

_____

_____

I am fasting for:

_____

_____

_____

_____

Listen and record His response to your prayers:

_____

_____

_____

_____

Fasting brings one into a deeper, more intimate,
and powerful relationship with the LORD.
—Jentezen Franklin

day six

As the deer pants for the water brooks So my soul pants for you, O God. My soul thirsts for God, for the living God. When shall I come and appear before God? My tears have been my food day and night, While they continually say to me, "Where is your God?" —Psalm 42:1-3 NKJV

Focus on the Word

Meditate on the Word of God. Record your thoughts or what you believe the scripture is speaking to you.

_____

_____

_____

_____

Activate Your Praise

Record your praise reports. Give God praise for who He is.

_____

_____

_____

_____

Record your thanks for what God has done in your life.

_____

_____

_____

_____

Search your heart

Search me, O God, and know my heart; Try me, and know my anxieties; And see if there is any wicked way in me, And lead me in the way everlasting. —Psalms 139:23-24 NKJV

Admit any sin in your life - your shortcomings, faults and disappointments.

_____

_____

_____

_____

Target your prayers
I am praying for:

_____

_____

_____

_____

I am fasting for:

_____

_____

_____

_____

Listen and record His response to your prayers:

_____

_____

_____

_____

Business as usual won't do. God's chosen prescription is fasting and praying until the powers of evil are defeated.
—John Kilpatrick,
When the Heavens are Brass

day seven

As the deer pants for the water brooks So my soul pants for you, O God. My soul thirsts for God, for the living God. When shall I come and appear before God? My tears have been my food day and night, While they continually say to me, "Where is your God?" —Psalm 42:1-3 NKJV

Focus on the Word

Meditate on the Word of God. Record your thoughts or what you believe the scripture is speaking to you.

_____

_____

_____

_____

Activate Your Praise

Record your praise reports. Give God praise for who He is.

_____

_____

_____

_____

Record your thanks for what God has done in your life.

_____

_____

_____

_____

Search your heart

Search me, O God, and know my heart; Try me, and know my anxieties; And see if there is any wicked way in me, And lead me in the way everlasting. —Psalms 139:23-24 NKJV

Admit any sin in your life - your shortcomings, faults and disappointments.

_____
_____
_____
_____

Target your prayers

I am praying for:

_____
_____
_____
_____

I am fasting for:

_____
_____
_____
_____

Listen and record His response to your prayers:

_____
_____
_____
_____

Is not this the fast that I choose? says the Lord.
—Isaiah 58:6 KJV

Dethroning king stomach

*I have not departed from the
commandment of His lips;
I have treasured the words of His mouth
more than necessary food.*

—Job 23:12 NKJV

VIEWPOINTS

By this point in your journey, you will have discovered first hand that there truly is a "dictator within" and his name is King Stomach. The only problem is that while this tyrant may be A king, he is not THE king and certainly not YOUR king. Just as you serve a much higher Authority, so also is your commitment to this period of fasting serving a much higher purpose than any amount of food could ever produce. Know that God sees your heart, treasures your sacrifice, and is ready to do a work in your life unlike any He has done before. Breakthroughs are in the offering, abundance is waiting to be released and victory is yours for the asking if you will continue to remain faithful. He will provide the grace to endure, but only you can dethrone that "dictator within". I challenge you to become a part of a small group and walk through this journey with accountability, encouragement and support from God's family. It is my prayer that you draw strength from one another and that you truly experience the power in fellowship with the Body of Christ.

Jentezen Franklin

"Therefore go…" Jesus says. God is with you…and so am I." So are the saints and pioneers of faith down through the ages. And they're all saying—shouting—You can do it, in Jesus' mighty name! Go for it! Think big! Dream without boundaries! Be limited only by what He limits. Change the world!

Bill Bright
Founder, Campus Crusade for Christ
Amazing Faith, the Authorized
Biography of Bill Bright

The purpose for week 2:

Week 2 focuses on Chapters Two and Three in your Fasting book. In these two powerful sections, we examine the mental, physical and spiritual battle we encounter as we war with "King Stomach." There are many crucial steps in your fast and this chapter offers practical "how to's" to help you through those tough spots. Scripture is filled with individuals who had to choose between the desires of the flesh and the disciplined life in pursuit of spiritual blessing and supernatural insight. In Chapter Three, we examine the three types of fasts; absolute, normal, and partial, and their biblical origins. The greatest message of these two chapters is that tremendous power and supernatural blessing await those who will forsake flesh for the chance to know their Savior and hear His voice.

By the end of this week you will:

Have a clearer understanding of the battle that rages between the carnal and the spirit man.

Examine the many ways God is moving "in" and "through" you.

Commit again to speaking regularly with accountability partners from your group.

Notes:

_____

_____

_____

_____

_____

_____

_____

_____

Key Principle:

Once you make the decision to fast, even if it's just for a day, God sees the desire of your heart. He will provide you the grace to endure and the breakthroughs you need to come to pass.

Group Discussion: Questions

Q 1 Describe "King Stomach" in your personal experience thus far:

_____

_____

_____

_____

Q 2 Describe other "physical" experiences since you began your fast:

_____

_____

_____

_____

Q 3 Describe any "spiritual" experiences since you began your fast:

_____

_____

_____

_____

Q 4 Describe what you feel God is doing "in" you as a result of your fasting:

_____

_____

_____

_____

Describe what you feel God is doing " through" you as a result of this experience:

_____

_____

_____

_____

Additional notes:

Steps of action:

Commit to continue speaking daily with your accountability partners as you enter the next phase of your fast.

Commit to being faithful in your daily prayer life by having a designated prayer time and place.

Take time daily to record your experiences in your prayer journal.

Make at least two phone calls this week to members of your small group to encourage them in the journey.

Final Thoughts:

Remember, whenever you begin a fast, if it doesn't mean anything to you, it won't mean anything to God. Fasting is little more than dieting unless combined with prayer and meditation on the Word. God sees the desires of your heart and He will provide you with the grace to endure and see the breakthroughs that you need…but you must dethrone that "dictator within"…King Stomach.

For further study: Luke 4:1-2; Numbers 11:4-7, 18-20
Exodus 34:27-28; Ezekiel 16:49-50; Matthew 6:33; Esther 4-7
Hebrews 12:15-17; Job 23:12

day one

I have not departed from the commandment of His lips; I have treasured the words of His mouth more than my necessary food. —Job 23:12 NKJV

Focus on the Word

Meditate on the Word of God. Record your thoughts or what you believe the scripture is speaking to you.

_____
_____
_____
_____

Activate Your Praise

Record your praise reports. Give God praise for who He is.

_____
_____
_____
_____

Record your thanks for what God has done in your life.

_____
_____
_____
_____

Search your heart

Search me, O God, and know my heart; Try me, and know my anxieties; And see if there is any wicked way in me, And lead me in the way everlasting. —Psalms 139:23-24 NKJV

Admit any sin in your life - your shortcomings, faults and disappointments.

_____

_____

_____

_____

Target your prayers

I am praying for:

_____

_____

_____

_____

I am fasting for:

_____

_____

_____

_____

Listen and record His response to your prayers:

_____

_____

_____

_____

When giving, praying and fasting are practiced together in the life of a believer, it creates a type of threefold cord that is not easily broken.
                              —_Jentezen Franklin_

day two

I have not departed from the commandment of His lips; I have treasured the words of His mouth more than my necessary food.   —Job 23:12 NKJV

Focus on the Word

Meditate on the Word of God. Record your thoughts or what you believe the scripture is speaking to you.

_____

_____

_____

_____

Activate Your Praise

Record your praise reports. Give God praise for who He is.

_____

_____

_____

_____

Record your thanks for what God has done in your life.

_____

_____

_____

_____

Search your heart

Search me, O God, and know my heart; Try me, and know my anxieties;
And see if there is any wicked way in me, And lead me in the way everlasting.
—Psalms 139:23-24 NKJV

Admit any sin in your life - your shortcomings, faults and disappointments.

_____

_____

_____

_____

Target your prayers

I am praying for:

_____

_____

_____

_____

I am fasting for:

_____

_____

_____

_____

Listen and record His response to your prayers:

_____

_____

_____

_____

Fasting is a discipline of the body with a tendency to humble the soul.
—Arthur Wallis, God's Chosen Fast

day three

I have not departed from the commandment of His lips; I have treasured the words of His mouth more than my necessary food. —Job 23:12 NKJV

Focus on the Word

Meditate on the Word of God. Record your thoughts or what you believe the scripture is speaking to you.

_____
_____
_____
_____

Activate Your Praise

Record your praise reports. Give God praise for who He is.

_____
_____
_____
_____

Record your thanks for what God has done in your life.

_____
_____
_____
_____

Search your heart

Search me, O God, and know my heart; Try me, and know my anxieties;
And see if there is any wicked way in me, And lead me in the way everlasting.
—Psalms 139:23-24 NKJV

Admit any sin in your life - your shortcomings, faults and disappointments.

_____

_____

_____

_____

Target your prayers

I am praying for:

_____

_____

_____

_____

I am fasting for:

_____

_____

_____

_____

Listen and record His response to your prayers:

_____

_____

_____

_____

"I proclaimed a fast there, at the river Ahava, that we might humble ourselves before our God."
                                    —*Ezra 8:21*

day four

I have not departed from the commandment of His lips; I have treasured the words of His mouth more than my necessary food.   —Job 23:12 NKJV

Focus on the Word

Meditate on the Word of God. Record your thoughts or what you believe the scripture is speaking to you.

_____

_____

_____

_____

Activate Your Praise

Record your praise reports. Give God praise for who He is.

_____

_____

_____

_____

Record your thanks for what God has done in your life.

_____

_____

_____

_____

Search your heart

Search me, O God, and know my heart; Try me, and know my anxieties;
And see if there is any wicked way in me, And lead me in the way everlasting.
—Psalms 139:23-24 NKJV

Admit any sin in your life - your shortcomings, faults and disappointments.

_____

_____

_____

_____

Target your prayers

I am praying for:

_____

_____

_____

_____

I am fasting for:

_____

_____

_____

_____

Listen and record His response to your prayers:

_____

_____

_____

_____

_Spirit-led prayer and fasting is so important because it turns our eyes
from ourselves, and our own cloudy skies, toward those things that
are on the heart of God._
—_John Kilpatrick, When the Heavens are Brass_

day five

I have not departed from the commandment of His lips; I have treasured the words of His mouth more than my necessary food. —Job 23:12 NKJV

Focus on the Word

Meditate on the Word of God. Record your thoughts or what you believe the scripture is speaking to you.

_____
_____
_____
_____

Activate Your Praise

Record your praise reports. Give God praise for who He is.

_____
_____
_____
_____

Record your thanks for what God has done in your life.

_____
_____
_____
_____

Search your heart

Search me, O God, and know my heart; Try me, and know my anxieties;
And see if there is any wicked way in me, And lead me in the way everlasting.
—Psalms 139:23-24 NKJV

Admit any sin in your life - your shortcomings, faults and disappointments.

_____

_____

_____

_____

Target your prayers
I am praying for:

_____

_____

_____

_____

I am fasting for:

_____

_____

_____

_____

Listen and record His response to your prayers:

_____

_____

_____

_____

"Now, therefore," says the Lord, "turn to Me with all your heart,
with fasting, with weeping, and with mourning".
                    —Joel 2:12

day six

I have not departed from the commandment of His lips; I have treasured the words of His mouth more than my necessary food. —*Job 23:12 NKJV*

Focus on the Word

Meditate on the Word of God. Record your thoughts or what you believe the scripture is speaking to you.

_____

_____

_____

_____

Activate Your Praise

Record your praise reports. Give God praise for who He is.

_____

_____

_____

_____

Record your thanks for what God has done in your life.

_____

_____

_____

_____

Search your heart

Search me, O God, and know my heart; Try me, and know my anxieties;
And see if there is any wicked way in me, And lead me in the way everlasting.
—*Psalms 139:23-24 NKJV*

Admit any sin in your life - your shortcomings, faults and disappointments.

_____
_____
_____
_____

Target your prayers
I am praying for:

_____
_____
_____
_____

I am fasting for:

_____
_____
_____
_____

Listen and record His response to your prayers:

_____
_____
_____
_____

They ministered unto the Lord, and fasted.
                    —Acts 13:2

day seven

I have not departed from the commandment of His lips; I have treasured the words of His mouth more than my necessary food.   —Job 23:12 NKJV

Focus on the Word

Meditate on the Word of God. Record your thoughts or what you believe the scripture is speaking to you.

_____

_____

_____

_____

Activate Your Praise

Record your praise reports. Give God praise for who He is.

_____

_____

_____

_____

Record your thanks for what God has done in your life.

_____

_____

_____

_____

Search your heart

Search me, O God, and know my heart; Try me, and know my anxieties;
And see if there is any wicked way in me, And lead me in the way everlasting.
—Psalms 139:23-24 NKJV

Admit any sin in your life - your shortcomings, faults and disappointments.

_____

_____

_____

_____

Target your prayers

I am praying for:

_____

_____

_____

_____

I am fasting for:

_____

_____

_____

_____

Listen and record His response to your prayers:

_____

_____

_____

_____

_Once you make that decision to fast...God sees the desire of your heart.
He will provide you with the grace to endure and see the breakthroughs
you need come to pass._

—Jentezen Franklin

Every assignment has a birthplace

My sheep hear my voice,
And I know them,
And they follow me:
And I give unto them eternal life;
And they shall never perish,
Neither shall any man
Pluck them out of your hand.

—John 10:27-28

Do you want to hear the voice of the Creator? Do you want to know Jesus more intimately? Do you want to know the direction He desires for you to take? I do. I am convinced that we will never walk in the perfect will of God until we seek Him through fasting. God looks throughout the earth for those faithful few upon whom He can pour out His blessing in extraordinary ways. God wants to use you in ways you cannot begin to imagine. All He is looking for is a life completely focused on Him. When you fast, you attract His attention as one willing to journey beyond the norms of religion and into the great adventure. God knows your hunger…but He also knows that you need Living Water and the Bread of Life. Taste and see that the Lord is good!

Jentezen Franklin

We are made neither for dreamless sleep nor dreamless lives. Dream on. Do not fear that your dream will go unfilled. Hold on to your dream, and let it hold on to you. Joseph knew terror in the pit and frustration in the prison, but he never lost his dream. In seasons of frustrating delays or hideous opposition, dream on.

Mark Rutland
Dream

The purpose for week 3:

Every assignment has a birth place. Every assignment, every call of God, every direction from Him starts somewhere. God has specific assignments for your life. How will you discover them? How will you hear His voice? How will you know His will and plans for your life? Fasting keeps you sensitive to His Spirit and incredibly attentive to His work in and around you. By now, you are a few weeks into your fast. The end is in sight, and while you may be at a turning point spiritually, these last days will bring more temptation than you experienced in the beginning. Stay the course. Be encouraged, and know that an anointing awaits the one who will pray and fast before his or her God and King.

By the end of this week you will:

Begin to trace the hand of God as He places within you your God-given assignments and continues to develop you for them.

Discover that many of the major movements of God came immediately following a season of prayer and fasting.

Begin to grasp what it means to present your body as a living sacrifice through your time of fasting.

See and hear that God is moving in the life of others in your group as they share the breakthroughs they are experiencing.

Notes:

_____

_____

_____

_____

_____

_____

_____

Key Principle:

Scripture says to, "present your bodies as a living sacrifice, holy, acceptable to God, which is your reasonable service." When you honor and worship God by presenting your body in this way through fasting, you too will know His assignments for your life.

"I am convinced that we will never walk in the perfect will of
God until we seek Him through fasting."

—*Jentezen Franklin*

Group Discussion: Questions

 Which stage of discovering your assignment from God are you in today? If you know what your assignment is, please write it below and share it with the group.

_____

_____

_____

_____

 Describe the movement of God in your life as He is preparing and equipping you for your assignment or moving you along in your search:

_____

_____

_____

_____

Please list and share with the group specific questions you have asked or are asking God in this period of fasting:

_____

_____

_____

_____

Please list and share any specific questions the Lord has answered during this time of fasting and praying:

_____

_____

_____

_____

Please describe any other movements of God that you have experienced these last three weeks:

_____

_____

_____

_____

Additional notes:

Steps of action:

Commit to continue to speak with your accountability partners as you enter the next phase of your fast.

Commit to being faithful in your daily prayer life by having a designated prayer time and place.

Take time daily to record your experiences in your prayer journal.

Make at least two phone calls this week to members of your small group to encourage them in the journey.

Final Thoughts:

Remember, Paul was fasting when God called him and shared the assignment for his life. Peter was fasting on the rooftop when God gave him a new revelation and called him to take the gospel to the Gentiles. Fasting prepares the way for God to give you fresh revelations, fresh visions, and clear purpose. God will do this for you. Stay the course and finish the race. An incredible reward of fresh wind and fresh fire awaits you on the other side.

For further study: Acts 9:7-9; Ephesians 5:8-10; Acts 10

Matthew 12:24; Joel 2:28-29; Jonah 3; John 10:10, 27-28; II Chronicles 7:14
Romans 12:1-2; Daniel 10:3; II Chronicles 7:14 & 20:2-4, 13-17
Mark 1:13 & 2:22

day one

My sheep hear my voice, And I know them, And they follow me: And I give unto them eternal life; And they shall never perish, Neither shall any man Pluck them out of your hand. —John 10:27-28

Focus on the Word

Meditate on the Word of God. Record your thoughts or what you believe the scripture is speaking to you.

_____
_____
_____
_____

Activate Your Praise

Record your praise reports. Give God praise for who He is.

_____
_____
_____
_____

Record your thanks for what God has done in your life.

_____
_____
_____
_____

Search your heart

Search me, O God, and know my heart; Try me, and know my anxieties;
And see if there is any wicked way in me, And lead me in the way everlasting.
—Psalms 139:23-24 NKJV

Admit any sin in your life - your shortcomings, faults and disappointments.

_____
_____
_____
_____

Target your prayers

I am praying for:

_____
_____
_____
_____

I am fasting for:

_____
_____
_____
_____

Listen and record His response to your prayers:

_____
_____
_____
_____

Fasting is found throughout the Bible. It always seems to show up when ordinary men need extraordinary power, provision, and perseverance to overcome impossible odds, enemies, or obstructions.
> *—Mahesh Chavda,*
> *The Hidden Power of Prayer and Fasting*

day two

My sheep hear my voice, And I know them, And they follow me: And I give unto them eternal life; And they shall never perish, Neither shall any man Pluck them out of your hand.   —John 10:27-28

Focus on the Word

Meditate on the Word of God. Record your thoughts or what you believe the scripture is speaking to you.

_____

_____

_____

_____

Activate Your Praise

Record your praise reports. Give God praise for who He is.

_____

_____

_____

_____

Record your thanks for what God has done in your life.

_____

_____

_____

_____

Search your heart

Search me, O God, and know my heart; Try me, and know my anxieties;
And see if there is any wicked way in me, And lead me in the way everlasting.
—Psalms 139:23-24 NKJV

Admit any sin in your life - your shortcomings, faults and disappointments.

_____
_____
_____
_____

Target your prayers

I am praying for:

_____
_____
_____
_____

I am fasting for:

_____
_____
_____
_____

Listen and record His response to your prayers:

_____
_____
_____
_____

_The most natural thing for us to do is to eat. When we give up eating,
we are deliberately turning away from the natural by turning to God and to
the supernatural. This has a deep significance._
—Derek Prince, Fasting

day three

My sheep hear my voice, And I know them, And they follow me: And I give unto them eternal life; And they shall never perish, Neither shall any man Pluck them out of your hand. —*John 10:27-28*

Focus on the Word

Meditate on the Word of God. Record your thoughts or what you believe the scripture is speaking to you.

_____

_____

_____

_____

Activate Your Praise

Record your praise reports. Give God praise for who He is.

_____

_____

_____

_____

Record your thanks for what God has done in your life.

_____

_____

_____

_____

Search your heart

Search me, O God, and know my heart; Try me, and know my anxieties; And see if there is any wicked way in me, And lead me in the way everlasting. —*Psalms 139:23-24 NKJV*

Admit any sin in your life - your shortcomings, faults and disappointments.

_____

_____

_____

_____

Target your prayers
I am praying for:

_____

_____

_____

_____

I am fasting for:

_____

_____

_____

_____

Listen and record His response to your prayers:

_____

_____

_____

_____

_The humbling experience of denying oneself food, strengthens your character
by self discipline and gives you a feeling of well being, a lighter step, a clearer eye,
a sharper brain, and also a higher endurance level and greater efficiency
for work and activity._

—Lillie R. Pearson, Fasting

day four

My sheep hear my voice, And I know them, And they follow me: And I give unto them eternal life; And they shall never perish, Neither shall any man Pluck them out of your hand. —John 10:27-28

Focus on the Word

Meditate on the Word of God. Record your thoughts or what you believe the scripture is speaking to you.

_____

_____

_____

_____

Activate Your Praise

Record your praise reports. Give God praise for who He is.

_____

_____

_____

_____

Record your thanks for what God has done in your life.

_____

_____

_____

_____

Search your heart

Search me, O God, and know my heart; Try me, and know my anxieties;
And see if there is any wicked way in me, And lead me in the way everlasting.
—Psalms 139:23-24 NKJV

Admit any sin in your life - your shortcomings, faults and disappointments.

_____

_____

_____

_____

Target your prayers
I am praying for:

_____

_____

_____

_____

I am fasting for:

_____

_____

_____

_____

Listen and record His response to your prayers:

_____

_____

_____

_____

Fasting and prayer will not only bind up your unbelief; it will also break the powers of darkness.
                    —Marilyn Hickey, Fasting and Prayer

day five

My sheep hear my voice, And I know them, And they follow me: And I give unto them eternal life; And they shall never perish, Neither shall any man Pluck them out of your hand.   —John 10:27-28

Focus on the Word

Meditate on the Word of God. Record your thoughts or what you believe the scripture is speaking to you.

_____
_____
_____
_____

Activate Your Praise

Record your praise reports. Give God praise for who He is.

_____
_____
_____
_____

Record your thanks for what God has done in your life.

_____
_____
_____
_____

Search your heart

Search me, O God, and know my heart; Try me, and know my anxieties;
And see if there is any wicked way in me, And lead me in the way everlasting.
—Psalms 139:23-24 NKJV

Admit any sin in your life - your shortcomings, faults and disappointments.

_____

_____

_____

_____

Target your prayers
I am praying for:

_____

_____

_____

_____

I am fasting for:

_____

_____

_____

_____

Listen and record His response to your prayers:

_____

_____

_____

_____

Since the days of Genesis, the effects of prayer and fasting have produced humility, promoted spiritual maturity and deepened relationships with God.
> —*Ted Haggard,*
> *Liberation Through Prayer and Fasting*

day six

My sheep hear my voice, And I know them, And they follow me: And I give unto them eternal life; And they shall never perish, Neither shall any man Pluck them out of your hand.   —John 10:27-28

Focus on the Word

Meditate on the Word of God. Record your thoughts or what you believe the scripture is speaking to you.

_____
_____
_____
_____

Activate Your Praise

Record your praise reports. Give God praise for who He is.

_____
_____
_____
_____

Record your thanks for what God has done in your life.

_____
_____
_____
_____

Search your heart

Search me, O God, and know my heart; Try me, and know my anxieties;
And see if there is any wicked way in me, And lead me in the way everlasting.
—Psalms 139:23-24 NKJV

Admit any sin in your life - your shortcomings, faults and disappointments.

_____
_____
_____
_____

Target your prayers

I am praying for:

_____
_____
_____
_____

I am fasting for:

_____
_____
_____
_____

Listen and record His response to your prayers:

_____
_____
_____
_____

Next, Jesus was taken into the wild by the Spirit for the Test.
The Devil was ready to give it. Jesus prepared for the Test by fasting
forty days and forty nights.
                              —Matt 4:1-2 (MSG)

day seven

My sheep hear my voice, And I know them, And they follow me: And I give unto them eternal life; And they shall never perish, Neither shall any man Pluck them out of your hand. —John 10:27-28

Focus on the Word

Meditate on the Word of God. Record your thoughts or what you believe the scripture is speaking to you.

_____

_____

_____

_____

Activate Your Praise

Record your praise reports. Give God praise for who He is.

_____

_____

_____

_____

Record your thanks for what God has done in your life.

_____

_____

_____

_____

Search your heart

Search me, O God, and know my heart; Try me, and know my anxieties;
And see if there is any wicked way in me, And lead me in the way everlasting.
—Psalms 139:23-24 NKJV

Admit any sin in your life - your shortcomings, faults and disappointments.

_____

_____

_____

_____

Target your prayers
I am praying for:

_____

_____

_____

_____

I am fasting for:

_____

_____

_____

_____

Listen and record His response to your prayers:

_____

_____

_____

_____

Fasting in secret gives you temperance and sobriety to watch, listen and wait, expecting great spiritual awareness in God as you fast.
—Lillie R. Pearson, Fasting

WEEK

Magnification...
the purest worship

*If my people who are called
by name will humble themselves and pray,
and seek my face, and turn from their wicked ways,
then will I hear from heaven, and will forgive their
sin and heal their land.*

—II Chronicles 7:14 (NKJV)

Magnify the Lord! If you are in a rut or routine where your worship isn't cutting it...if you have not heard God speak to you in a long time...if your circumstances seem to be the biggest obstacle in your life...stop everything and begin a fast. It does not matter what you fast or how long. The details are not as important as your heart's desire to satisfy and magnify God with your worship and sacrifice. Fasting and praying will provide the perspective of God that can only be described as magnification. Through this, His perfect will, His presence, and His power will come into focus with greater clarity than you ever thought possible. Stay the course...finish the race...continue to present your body as a living sacrifice and see the Lord open the windows of Heaven to you and shower you with His presence.

Jentezen Franklin

Worship is a deliberate, steady, focused time with God. Worship anticipates not only an encounter with God, but also a clear, next word from God. Worship is totally God-centered! God Focused! Out of worship comes a clearer and more focused relationship of faith and obedience with God. Worship is God's way of developing character and directing the life into the center of His will. Worship always has enormous opportunities for God, in His own time, to reveal Himself and His immediate purposes to those He has chosen to be His special servants.

Henry Blackaby,
Created to be God's Friend

The purpose for week 4:

When we don't do what it takes to stay sharp and sensitive to the Holy Spirit, our praise, worship, offerings, and even preaching can become heartless routines to God. God desires to move powerfully in your life. Fasting is a form of worship. It will humble you, remind you of your dependency on God and bring you back to your first love. It causes you to magnify Him as you wait on Him to supply you with the Bread of life.

By the end of this week you will:

Have completed most, if not all of your fast..

Begin to understand and experience the concepts of "magnification" and "worship" in a fresh new way.

Begin to understand, through dialogue and personal experience, what it means to be "desperate" for more of God.

Experience, first hand, the bond that exists between you and your small group family as you have developed a network of accountability and friendship.

Notes:

_____

_____

_____

_____

_____

Key Principle:

There are dimensions of our glorious King that will never be revealed to the casual disinterested worshiper. There are walls of intercession that will never be scaled by dispassionate religious service. When you take steps to break out of the ordinary and worship Him as He deserves, you will begin to see facets of His being that you never knew existed. He will begin to share secrets with you about Himself, His plans and His desires for you. When you worship God as He deserves He is magnified.

Group Discussion: Questions

 Have you experienced any significant breakthroughs this past week? If yes, please list and share them with the group.

_____

_____

_____

_____

 How would you describe your times of "worship" since you have begun fasting and praying?

_____

_____

_____

_____

Pastor Franklin states, in the text, "Magnification didn't make that object any bigger than it actually was, but it greatly enlarged my view, allowing me to see details that were hidden without magnification." Who or what has been "magnified" in your life since you began your time of fasting and praying?

_____

_____

_____

_____

Please take a moment to list and share with the group how you get through each day and what specifically has sustained you through this period of physical and spiritual challenge?

_____

_____

_____

The text, in chapters six and seven, makes several references to the "presence" of God. In your time of fasting and praying, have you experienced a "breaking through to more of His presence?" If so, please try to describe this and explain how it has affected your experience.

_____

_____

_____

_____

Steps of action:

Commit to continue to speak with your accountability partners as you enter the next phase of your fast.

Commit to being faithful in your daily prayer life by having a designated prayer time and place.

Take time daily to record your experiences in your prayer journal.

Make at least two phone calls this week to members of your small group to encourage them in the journey.

Final Thoughts:

We must arrive at the place where we are desperate for God again. We must begin to desire Him more than food or drink. Let us be filled with the Bread of Presence instead of the refuse of religion. Begin to make fasting a regular discipline, and see how God answers your hunger.

For further study: Psalms 50:12-15; John 4:6-34

John 4:6-34; Acts 10; Romans 12:1; Matthew 4-6; Matthew 8:5-13
Palms 34; Mark 7:25-30; Matthew 12:1-8

day one

It is written, Man shall not live by bread alone, but by every word that proceedeth out of the mouth of God.   —Matthew 4:4

Focus on the Word

Meditate on the Word of God. Record your thoughts or what you believe the scripture is speaking to you.

_____

_____

_____

_____

Activate Your Praise

Record your praise reports. Give God praise for who He is.

_____

_____

_____

_____

Record your thanks for what God has done in your life.

_____

_____

_____

_____

Search your heart

Search me, O God, and know my heart; Try me, and know my anxieties;
And see if there is any wicked way in me, And lead me in the way everlasting.
*   —Psalms 139:23-24 NKJV*

Admit any sin in your life - your shortcomings, faults and disappointments.

_____
_____
_____
_____

Target your prayers
I am praying for:

_____
_____
_____
_____

I am fasting for:

_____
_____
_____
_____

Listen and record His response to your prayers:

_____
_____
_____
_____

Fasting prepares you for a new anointing. God can't put that kind of wine in old skins. If you want new wine, new miracles, new closeness, new intimacy with Him, then it's time to call a fast and shed that old skin for the new.
—Jentezen Franklin

day two

It is written, Man shall not live by bread alone, but by every word that proceedeth out of the mouth of God. —Matthew 4:4

Focus on the Word

Meditate on the Word of God. Record your thoughts or what you believe the scripture is speaking to you.

_____

_____

_____

_____

Activate Your Praise

Record your praise reports. Give God praise for who He is.

_____

_____

_____

_____

Record your thanks for what God has done in your life.

_____

_____

_____

_____

Search your heart

Search me, O God, and know my heart; Try me, and know my anxieties;
And see if there is any wicked way in me, And lead me in the way everlasting.
—Psalms 139:23-24 NKJV

Admit any sin in your life - your shortcomings, faults and disappointments.

_____

_____

_____

_____

Target your prayers

I am praying for:

_____

_____

_____

_____

I am fasting for:

_____

_____

_____

_____

Listen and record His response to your prayers:

_____

_____

_____

_____

Is this not the fast which I choose, To loosen the bonds of wickedness,
To undo the bands of the yoke, And to let the oppressed go free And break
every yoke?
                    —*Isaiah 58:6 (NASB)*

day three

It is written, Man shall not live by bread alone, but by every word that proceedeth out of the mouth of God.   —Matthew 4:4

Focus on the Word

Meditate on the Word of God. Record your thoughts or what you believe the scripture is speaking to you.

_____
_____
_____
_____

Activate Your Praise

Record your praise reports. Give God praise for who He is.

_____
_____
_____
_____

Record your thanks for what God has done in your life.

_____
_____
_____
_____

Search your heart

Search me, O God, and know my heart; Try me, and know my anxieties;
And see if there is any wicked way in me, And lead me in the way everlasting.
—Psalms 139:23-24 NKJV

Admit any sin in your life - your shortcomings, faults and disappointments.

_____

_____

_____

_____

Target your prayers

I am praying for:

_____

_____

_____

_____

I am fasting for:

_____

_____

_____

_____

Listen and record His response to your prayers:

_____

_____

_____

_____

When combined, these two activities (prayer and fasting) are
among the most successful tools for maintaining a steady walk with the Lord.
—Ted Haggard

day four

It is written, Man shall not live by bread alone, but by every word that proceedeth out of the mouth of God. —Matthew 4:4

Focus on the Word

Meditate on the Word of God. Record your thoughts or what you believe the scripture is speaking to you.

_____

_____

_____

_____

Activate Your Praise

Record your praise reports. Give God praise for who He is.

_____

_____

_____

_____

Record your thanks for what God has done in your life.

_____

_____

_____

_____

Search your heart

Search me, O God, and know my heart; Try me, and know my anxieties;
And see if there is any wicked way in me, And lead me in the way everlasting.
—Psalms 139:23-24 NKJV

Admit any sin in your life - your shortcomings, faults and disappointments.

_____

_____

_____

_____

Target your prayers

I am praying for:

_____

_____

_____

_____

I am fasting for:

_____

_____

_____

_____

Listen and record His response to your prayers:

_____

_____

_____

_____

Be still, and know that I am God.
                              —Psalms 46:10 (NKJV)

day five

It is written, Man shall not live by bread alone, but by every word that proceedeth out of the mouth of God.   —Matthew 4:4

Focus on the Word

Meditate on the Word of God. Record your thoughts or what you believe the scripture is speaking to you.

_____

_____

_____

_____

Activate Your Praise

Record your praise reports. Give God praise for who He is.

_____

_____

_____

_____

Record your thanks for what God has done in your life.

_____

_____

_____

_____

Search your heart

Search me, O God, and know my heart; Try me, and know my anxieties;
And see if there is any wicked way in me, And lead me in the way everlasting.
—Psalms 139:23-24 NKJV

Admit any sin in your life - your shortcomings, faults and disappointments.

_____

_____

_____

_____

Target your prayers

I am praying for:

_____

_____

_____

_____

I am fasting for:

_____

_____

_____

_____

Listen and record His response to your prayers:

_____

_____

_____

_____

But the time will come when the bridegroom will be taken from them,
and on that day they will fast.
                    —Mark 2:20

day six

It is written, Man shall not live by bread alone, but by every word that proceedeth out of the mouth of God.   —Matthew 4:4

Focus on the Word

Meditate on the Word of God. Record your thoughts or what you believe the scripture is speaking to you.

_____
_____
_____
_____

Activate Your Praise

Record your praise reports. Give God praise for who He is.

_____
_____
_____
_____

Record your thanks for what God has done in your life.

_____
_____
_____
_____

Search your heart

Search me, O God, and know my heart; Try me, and know my anxieties;
And see if there is any wicked way in me, And lead me in the way everlasting.
—Psalms 139:23-24 NKJV

Admit any sin in your life - your shortcomings, faults and disappointments.

_____
_____
_____
_____

Target your prayers
I am praying for:

_____
_____
_____
_____

I am fasting for:

_____
_____
_____
_____

Listen and record His response to your prayers:

_____
_____
_____
_____

It is evident that fasting is not a religious duty or form, and certainly does not force God to notice and issue or grant His favor (Isaiah 58:4). Rather, it creates changes in us that make it possible for us to interact with God.
      —_Ted Haggard_

day seven

It is written, Man shall not live by bread alone, but by every word that proceedeth out of the mouth of God. —Matthew 4:4

Focus on the Word

Meditate on the Word of God. Record your thoughts or what you believe the scripture is speaking to you.

_____

_____

_____

_____

Activate Your Praise

Record your praise reports. Give God praise for who He is.

_____

_____

_____

_____

Record your thanks for what God has done in your life.

_____

_____

_____

_____

Search your heart

Search me, O God, and know my heart; Try me, and know my anxieties;
And see if there is any wicked way in me, And lead me in the way everlasting.
—Psalms 139:23-24 NKJV

Admit any sin in your life - your shortcomings, faults and disappointments.

_____

_____

_____

_____

Target your prayers

I am praying for:

_____

_____

_____

_____

I am fasting for:

_____

_____

_____

_____

Listen and record His response to your prayers:

_____

_____

_____

_____

Fasting has a way of detaching us from the world of the material so that our thinking becomes rightly orientated, focused on God and the unseen world of which He is the center.
                                   —*Arthur Wallis*

Rewarded openly... nothing shall be impossible

*Now therefore, if you will indeed obey My voice and keep
My covenant, then you shall be a special treasure
to Me above all people; for all the
earth is Mine. And you shall be to Me a kingdom
of priests and a holy nation."
These are the words which you shall speak
to the children of Israel.*

—Exodus 19:5-6

We must arrive at the place where we are desperate for God again. We must begin to desire Him more than food or drink. Let us be filled with the Bread of Presence instead of the refuse of religion. It is my prayer that you will make fasting a regular discipline. Scripture and church history are filled with accounts of the miracles that fasting has wrought in the church. It is also my sincerest belief that when fasting is a lifestyle, poverty will not be. I have seen people who have never fasted before experience marvelous breakthroughs in their lives. Your faithfulness during this time of fasting and prayer will bring supernatural blessings and release the power of God to overcome any situation. Purpose today to make fasting a regular part of your Christian walk and watch as the Lord comes in wonderful and miraculous ways.

Jentezen Franklin

This frightening hour calls aloud for men with the gift of prophetic insight. I am talking about His coming and possessing the full body and mind and life and heart, taking the whole personality over, gently but directly and bluntly, making it His, so that we may become a habitation of God through the Spirit.

A.W. Tozer
Gems from Tozer

The purpose for week 5:

The focus for week 5 is celebrating what God has done in and through you as a result of this time of prayer and fasting. The challenge for you today is to share your story. Your journey through this process has, no doubt, taken you places you have never been and hopefully brought you into a place of incredible blessing. Your story matters. God has done a wonderful thing for you and the challenge is now to take what He has done and multiply it into the lives of others. Many will be encouraged and strengthened through your story of faithfulness and by the testimony of your experiences. Prayerfully consider what you would be willing to share with others.

By the end of this week you will:

Begin to examine areas of unforgiveness and bitterness that the Lord is asking you to surrender to Him.

Have an opportunity to reflect on your fasting experience and to express to others the movement of God in and through you during this powerful time.

Have the opportunity to affirm, encourage and thank your small group family for their partnership throughout this remarkable journey.

Notes:

_____

_____

_____

_____

Key Principle:

True spiritual fasting is a private, personal discipline that the Lord rewards openly. Fasting brings great blessing and breakthroughs that can only be explained through the supernatural intervention of an all-seeing, all-knowing God. By this week, you have tasted of the Lord; you have counted on Him as your Bread of Life and found Him to be faithful.

Group Discussion: Questions

 The last two chapters of your text deal with the issues of forgiveness and overcoming bitterness. Has this area been a part of your fasting experience and if so, would you please share what God has done in and through you as it relates to these?

_____

_____

_____

_____

 Please rate your relationship with the Lord on a scale from 1-10, (10 being as good as it can possibly be, and a 1 being distant and far removed from God) (circle one)

1   2   3   4   5   6   7   8   9   10

Q3 Why did you choose the score that you did and what would it take to move it closer to a 10?

_____

_____

_____

_____

Please take a moment to list and share with the group how you get through each day and what specifically has sustained you through this period of physical and spiritual challenge?

_____

_____

_____

_____

The text, in chapters six and seven, makes several references to the "presence" of God. In your time of fasting and praying, have you experienced a "breaking through to more of His presence?" If so, please try to describe this and explain how it has affected your experience.

_____

_____

_____

_____

Additional notes:

Steps of action:

Prayerfully consider becoming involved in a Small Group at your church on a regular basis.

Commit to being faithful in your daily prayer life by having a designated prayer time and place.

Take time daily to finish recording your experiences in your prayer journal.

Make at least two phone calls this week to members of your small group to thank them for their support, love and encouragement in your journey.

Final Thoughts:

Fasting humbles and brings clarity, allowing you to get unforgiveness and bitterness out of your heart. It also helps you to be cleansed from within, in a spiritual sense, because it makes you sensitive to the desires of the Lord. Do not be surprised if your fasting has done such a work in your life that the lost are drawn to you and to what God is doing in and through your life.

For further study: Genesis 15:1; Genesis 41:39-45

Joel 2:17; I Kings 3:10-13; Matthew 6:1-4; Daniel 6:1-4; Romans 12:1
Isaiah 58:8; Job 23:12; Matthew 17:21; Joel 2:15-16, 28; Judges 19:22, 26-48
II Chronicles 33:1-13; Psalms 69:30-32

day one

Do not be afraid, Abram. I am your shield, your exceedingly great reward.
—Genesis 15:1 NKJV.

Focus on the Word

Meditate on the Word of God. Record your thoughts or what you believe the scripture is speaking to you.

_____
_____
_____
_____

Activate Your Praise

Record your praise reports. Give God praise for who He is.

_____
_____
_____
_____

Record your thanks for what God has done in your life.

_____
_____
_____
_____

Search your heart

Search me, O God, and know my heart; Try me, and know my anxieties;
And see if there is any wicked way in me, And lead me in the way everlasting.
—Psalms 139:23-24 NKJV

Admit any sin in your life - your shortcomings, faults and disappointments.

_____
_____
_____
_____

Target your prayers
I am praying for:

_____
_____
_____
_____

I am fasting for:

_____
_____
_____
_____

Listen and record His response to your prayers:

_____
_____
_____
_____

She did not go out from the temple enclosure, but was worshiping night and day with fasting and prayer.
—Luke 2:37 (AMP)

day two

Do not be afraid, Abram. I am your shield, your exceedingly great reward.
—Genesis 15:1 NKJV.

Focus on the Word

Meditate on the Word of God. Record your thoughts or what you believe the scripture is speaking to you.

_____

_____

_____

_____

Activate Your Praise

Record your praise reports. Give God praise for who He is.

_____

_____

_____

_____

Record your thanks for what God has done in your life.

_____

_____

_____

_____

Search your heart

Search me, O God, and know my heart; Try me, and know my anxieties;
And see if there is any wicked way in me, And lead me in the way everlasting.
—Psalms 139:23-24 NKJV

Admit any sin in your life - your shortcomings, faults and disappointments.

_____
_____
_____
_____

Target your prayers
I am praying for:

_____
_____
_____
_____

I am fasting for:

_____
_____
_____
_____

Listen and record His response to your prayers:

_____
_____
_____
_____

When you hunger for God, He will break the rules of man and cause His Favor to come on your life.
—Jentezen Franklin

day three

Do not be afraid, Abram. I am your shield, your exceedingly great reward.
—Genesis 15:1 NKJV.

Focus on the Word

Meditate on the Word of God. Record your thoughts or what you believe the scripture is speaking to you.

Activate Your Praise

Record your praise reports. Give God praise for who He is.

Record your thanks for what God has done in your life.

Search your heart

Search me, O God, and know my heart; Try me, and know my anxieties;
And see if there is any wicked way in me, And lead me in the way everlasting.
—Psalms 139:23-24 NKJV

Admit any sin in your life - your shortcomings, faults and disappointments.

_____
_____
_____
_____

Target your prayers
I am praying for:

_____
_____
_____
_____

I am fasting for:

_____
_____
_____
_____

Listen and record His response to your prayers:

_____
_____
_____
_____

Intimacy with the Almighty calls for disciplines that are no longer valued or emulated by the majority today.
                              —*Charles Swindoll, Intimacy with the Almighty*

day four

Do not be afraid, Abram. I am your shield, your exceedingly great reward.
—Genesis 15:1 NKJV.

Focus on the Word

Meditate on the Word of God. Record your thoughts or what you believe the scripture is speaking to you.

_____

_____

_____

_____

Activate Your Praise

Record your praise reports. Give God praise for who He is.

_____

_____

_____

_____

Record your thanks for what God has done in your life.

_____

_____

_____

_____

Search your heart

Search me, O God, and know my heart; Try me, and know my anxieties;
And see if there is any wicked way in me, And lead me in the way everlasting.
—Psalms 139:23-24 NKJV

Admit any sin in your life - your shortcomings, faults and disappointments.

_____
_____
_____
_____

Target your prayers

I am praying for:

_____
_____
_____
_____

I am fasting for:

_____
_____
_____
_____

Listen and record His response to your prayers:

_____
_____
_____
_____

Fasting and prayer are twins. Don't divide them; keep them together, and you will have the most effective prayer life you have ever had.
                                        —Marilyn Hickey

day five

Do not be afraid, Abram. I am your shield, your exceedingly great reward.
—Genesis 15:1 NKJV.

Focus on the Word

Meditate on the Word of God. Record your thoughts or what you believe the scripture is speaking to you.

_____

_____

_____

_____

Activate Your Praise

Record your praise reports. Give God praise for who He is.

_____

_____

_____

_____

Record your thanks for what God has done in your life.

_____

_____

_____

_____

Search your heart

Search me, O God, and know my heart; Try me, and know my anxieties;
And see if there is any wicked way in me, And lead me in the way everlasting.
—Psalms 139:23-24 NKJV

Admit any sin in your life - your shortcomings, faults and disappointments.

_____
_____
_____
_____

Target your prayers
I am praying for:

_____
_____
_____
_____

I am fasting for:

_____
_____
_____
_____

Listen and record His response to your prayers:

_____
_____
_____
_____

And I set my face to the Lord God to seek Him by prayer and supplications,
with fasting and sackcloth and ashes; And I prayed to the Lord my God and
made confession…
                              —Dan 9:3-4 (AMP)

day six

Do not be afraid, Abram. I am your shield, your exceedingly great reward.
—Genesis 15:1 NKJV.

Focus on the Word

Meditate on the Word of God. Record your thoughts or what you believe the scripture is speaking to you.

_____
_____
_____
_____

Activate Your Praise

Record your praise reports. Give God praise for who He is.

_____
_____
_____
_____

Record your thanks for what God has done in your life.

_____
_____
_____
_____

Search your heart

Search me, O God, and know my heart; Try me, and know my anxieties;
And see if there is any wicked way in me, And lead me in the way everlasting.
—Psalms 139:23-24 NKJV

Admit any sin in your life - your shortcomings, faults and disappointments.

_____
_____
_____
_____

Target your prayers
I am praying for:

_____
_____
_____
_____

I am fasting for:

_____
_____
_____
_____

Listen and record His response to your prayers:

_____
_____
_____
_____

Man eats too much. Thus he lives on only a quarter of what he consumes.
The doctors, however, live on the remaining three-quarters.
                    —The Edwin Smith Papyrus

day seven

Do not be afraid, Abram. I am your shield, your exceedingly great reward.
—Genesis 15:1 NKJV.

Focus on the Word

Meditate on the Word of God. Record your thoughts or what you believe the scripture is speaking to you.

_____
_____
_____
_____

Activate Your Praise

Record your praise reports. Give God praise for who He is.

_____
_____
_____
_____

Record your thanks for what God has done in your life.

_____
_____
_____
_____

Search your heart

Search me, O God, and know my heart; Try me, and know my anxieties;
And see if there is any wicked way in me, And lead me in the way everlasting.
—Psalms 139:23-24 NKJV

Admit any sin in your life - your shortcomings, faults and disappointments.

_____
_____
_____
_____

Target your prayers
I am praying for:

_____
_____
_____
_____

I am fasting for:

_____
_____
_____
_____

Listen and record His response to your prayers:

_____
_____
_____
_____

What? Know ye not that your body is the temple of the Holy Ghost which is in you,
which ye have of God, and ye are not your own? For ye are bought with a price:
therefore glorify God in your body, and in your spirit, which are God's.
—I Corinthians 6:19-20

NOTES